T0199051

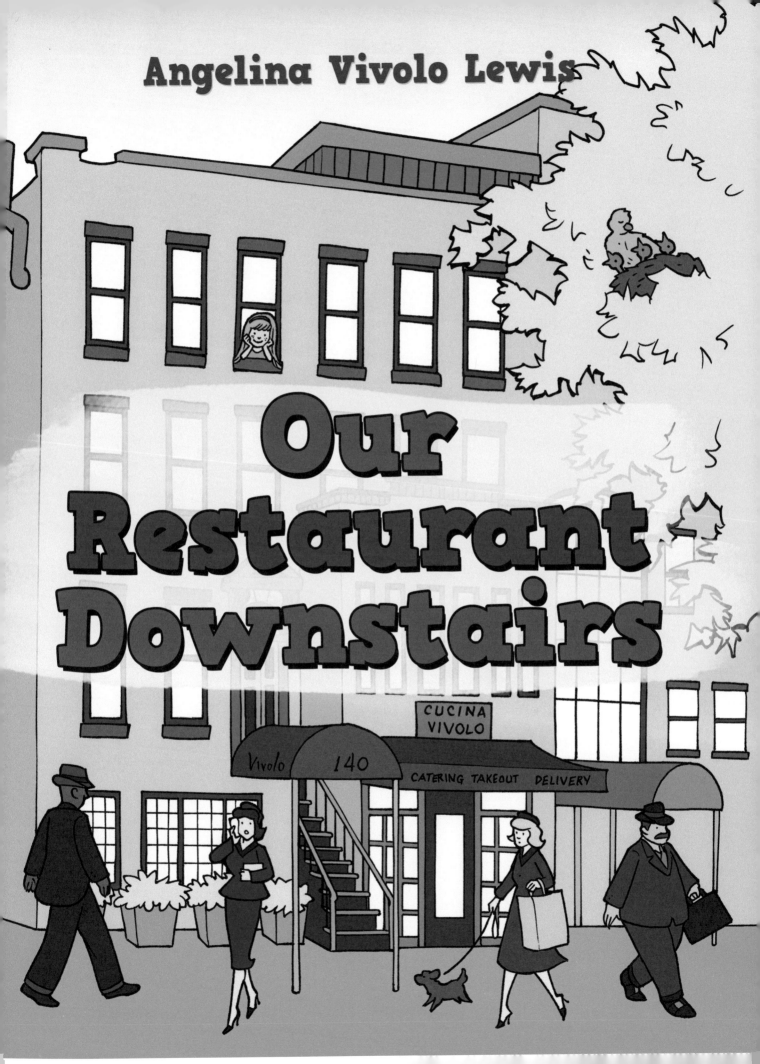

AuthorHouse™
1663 Liberty Drive
Bloomington, IN 47403
www.authorhouse.com
Phone: 1 (800) 839-8640

Published by AuthorHouse 11/29/2018

ISBN: 978-1-5462-6886-4 (sc)
ISBN: 978-1-5462-6885-7 (e)

Library of Congress Control Number: 2018913636

Print information available on the last page.

Any people depicted in stock imagery provided by Getty Images are models,
and such images are being used for illustrative purposes only.
Certain stock imagery © Getty Images.

This book is printed on acid-free paper.

authorHOUSE®

Our Restaurant Downstairs

I am Angie and I live in New York City. My Dad owns a restaurant and our family lives in the apartment upstairs. My bedroom is on the top floor. I look out the window and see people pass by on the city streets. I watch and wonder where everyone is rushing off to.

In the morning I run downstairs and see a big truck delivering fresh bread to the restaurant in tall brown paper bags. I grab a warm roll and eat it on the way to school.

After school, we walk home down Park Avenue. I see yellow taxi cabs, bright spring tulips and giant buildings. I see the doorman who works at the big apartment building we pass each day. He gives me a high five and says, "Have a good afternoon, young lady!"

We stop at the restaurant for an after-school snack. I sit at the end of the bar with Carmine, the maître d'. He asks me about school and makes me a Shirley Temple.

Dad brings me to the kitchen to talk to the chefs. We see them preparing the food. They are chopping the vegetables, carving the meat and filleting the fish. Rene, the head chef, gives me a taste of tomato sauce from the big brass pot and says, "Boun Appetito, Miss Angie!" It's delicious.

The waiters and chefs are on their break now. They sit together and have dinner at a long table. I hear laughing and talking as I head through the secret door that leads to our apartment upstairs. Next, the waiters will fold the napkins, set the tables and light the candles. It's almost 5 o'clock and the restaurant will open again for dinner.

I do my homework and play with my brothers. We pretend we have our own restaurant. I am the chef, my little brother is the waiter and my big brother is the maître d'. Mom says, "Let's see your maître d' smile!" He grins from ear to ear.

Dad comes upstairs for dinner. We talk about our day and have special time as a family. After dinner, he goes back to work in the restaurant.

Sometimes we sneak downstairs to see what's going on. I see men in suits and ladies in pretty dresses. If we're lucky, we catch a glimpse of a famous person eating dinner. Tonight we saw a baseball player and my brother asked, "Hey, aren't you Joe DiMaggio?" He laughed and we took a picture.

Another day has come and gone and it's time to go to sleep. Mom reads me a story and kisses me goodnight. I lie in my bed and listen to the sounds of the city. I hear cars driving by and trucks honking their horns. I hear the happy chatter of people outside the restaurant. I close my eyes as the sweet sounds of New York City soothe me to sleep. This is home.

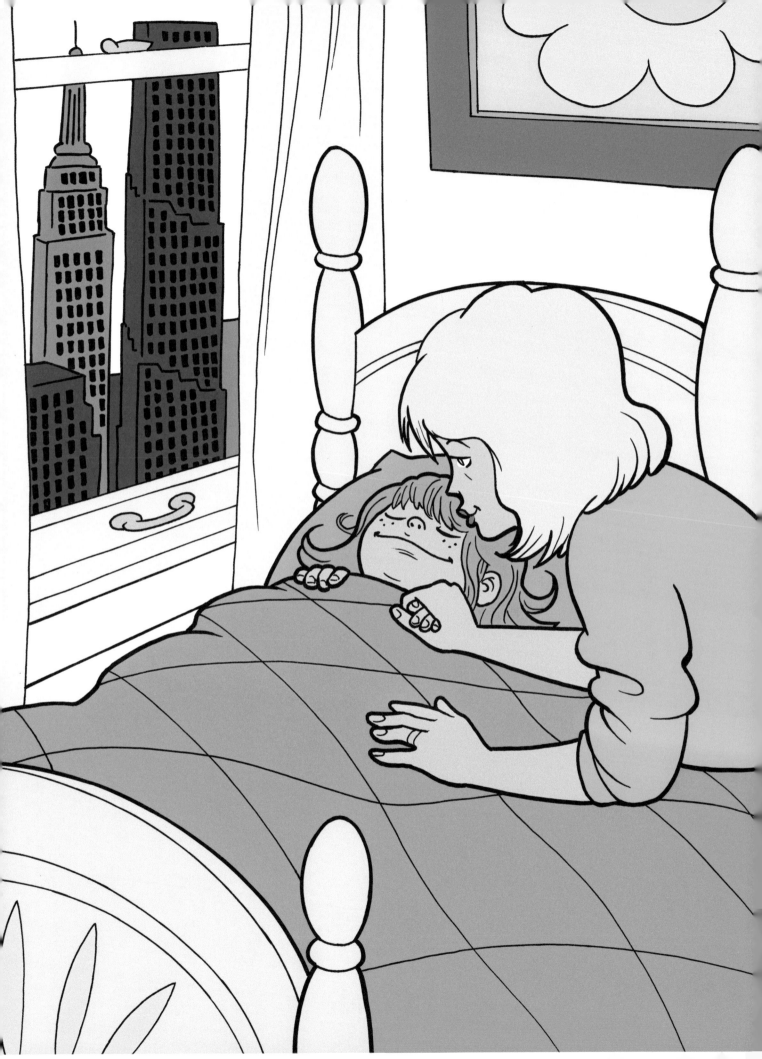

Printed in the United States
By Bookmasters